"The pressures of life s[illegible]stracted by the pain. How impo[illegible]eautiful devotions on the Psalr[illegible] eyes to the One who loves us most and leads us best. Packed with bite-sized reminders about the character and call of God, there's fuel here for every limping believer. A real spur to perseverance and hope."

Helen Thorne, Director of Training and Resources, Biblical Counselling UK

"Some of the deep treasures of scripture pass us by because we rush through our Bible reading. We too often find ourselves glancing at words, rather than pausing long enough to gaze into the heart of our God. This book is a reflective stroll through some well-loved psalms. It's pace is deliberately leisurely, enabling the reader to pause, and meditate upon the beauty and majesty of our unchanging God. I have been greatly blessed and pastorally encouraged by this book and commended it to all who seek to 'be still' before the Lord and simply marvel at Him."

Colin Webster, Minister at Cornerstone Church Nottingham

MATT SEARLES

BE STILL

PSALM DEVOTIONS

10 Publishing
a division of 10 of those.com

First published in Great Britain in 2021

British Library Cataloguing in Publication Data
A record for this book is available from the British Library

ISBN: 978-1-915705-16-7

Designed by Jude May
Cover image © CPD-Lab | iStock

Printed in Denmark by Nørhaven

10Publishing, a division of 10ofthose.com
Unit C, Tomlinson Road, Leyland, PR25 2DY, England
Email: info@10ofthose.com
Website: www.10ofthose.com

CONTENTS

INTRODUCTION

Be still before the Lord and wait patiently for him (Ps. 37:7).

Ours is a restless, rushed society. Life seems to move ever faster each year. We struggle to fit as much in as we can, and many of us rarely pause for reflection. Perhaps the same is true of our spiritual lives. We can so easily feel that our walk with the Lord is just one extra thing to squeeze into our crowded days and weeks.

But rather than the Lord being just another clamouring voice making demands on our time and energy, in fact he is the one who gives rest. He came to carry our burdens, not lay burdens on us. Psalm 37 has the repeated instruction 'fret not yourself'. Fretting and restless activity are the hallmarks of those who have no loving heavenly Father to provide for them. By contrast, David tells us, 'Be still before the Lord and wait patiently for him.'

These devotions are intended to help you do just that. Over the past year I've been more conscious of the need just to 'be still' before the Lord; to spend time meditating on a verse or two of Scripture, and to turn them back to him in prayer.

Thomas Brooks, a seventeenth-century church leader, described the importance of slowing down in this way:

Remember that it is not hasty reading but serious meditation on holy and heavenly truths, that makes them prove sweet and profitable to the soul. It is not the mere touching of the flower by the bee that gathers honey, but her abiding for a time on the flower that draws out the sweet. It is not he that reads most but he that meditates most that will prove to be the choicest, sweetest, wisest and strongest Christian.[1]

The devotions in this book are all short, focussing on just a verse or two. But each devotion is split into two or more sections, with a break marked 'Selah'. At this point, you may wish to pause to reflect and pray, or maybe even stop and resume the rest of the devotion another day.

My primary audience is those who are already followers of Jesus. We may be in very different circumstances to the original psalm writers, but we worship the same God, so *their* words can become *our* words, and we can learn from their experiences. The words of the psalmists can retune our hearts as we sing and pray along with them.

Of course, you may be reading this because you are looking into Christianity, or unsure of where you are on your journey of faith. I hope that you too will feel very welcome as you spend a little time with the psalmists, and see what life looks like through their eyes. The psalmists, like Christians today, are far from perfect and don't have all the answers. But they do testify to a God who is faithful, can be trusted and makes wonderful promises to his people. I hope that the presentation of the Christian life that these psalms give might make you want to come to know Jesus for yourself, and participate in the promises offered in these psalms.

I've chosen these four psalms because they lend themselves so naturally to being meditated on in small sections. But I hope that you'll take the principle of lingering on just one verse or image and apply this to other Scriptures, forming habits of meditating on God's word. Time with the Lord is not one more item on our 'to do' list, but rather a gift from God, the refreshment that our weary souls so desperately need. Be still before the Lord, and wait patiently for him.

1

PSALM 16:1 *Dependence*

Preserve me, O God, for in you I take refuge.

Psalm 16 is a beautiful example of what it means to have one's heart set on God. David pours out his heart to his Lord in prayer, and in so doing paints a portrait of the devoted life: dependence, delight, fellowship, turning from idols, contentment, security, hope and joy.

David is not doing this to shame or intimidate us, rather he is giving us an example to follow. These are words to grow into. David calls us to sing along with him, and allow the Lord to retune our hearts so that we grow more and more into these wonderful characteristics. You might want to skim the whole psalm now and think which aspect of David's devotion you find most appealing.

—Selah—

David begins the psalm by asking the Lord to preserve him – to keep him safe. These are words to cry out to God in times of deep distress, in affliction and in trial. These are words we would do well to learn and store in our heart for times when we need to cry out to God.

But in this psalm, these words aren't spoken in a time of distress. Rather, they find themselves in a warm, joyous psalm of devotion to God, sung by the worshipping congregation of Israel.

Even on our brightest days, we need the Lord's preservation. This psalm can help us remember that even when we *feel* we don't need God, he is nonetheless our sustainer and provider. We need him just as much on days of sunshine as on days of rain. We depend on him for everything, even every breath we take. These words foster our dependence on God. They remind us that we can't do life on our own.

'Preserve me, O God, for in you I take refuge' is a prayer on our days of 'strength' as well as on days when we know ourselves to be weak. We never move on from utter dependence on our Lord. As Jesus said, 'apart from me you can do nothing' (John 15:5).

—Selah—

Praying and singing these words is a reminder to us to look for refuge in God alone, not anywhere else. We may be tempted to look elsewhere for security and provision, but God is the only true refuge – and the only refuge we need.

These are words we could use to pray for others as well. We can use them to pray for God to watch over those we love: 'Lord, preserve Naomi today, for you are her refuge.' But we could also use them to pray for people to share the psalmist's perspective: 'Lord, may Naomi be like the psalmist today, and find her refuge in you. May she look to you in harder times, not look elsewhere.' I can think of few prayers I'd rather someone pray for me than this: that the Lord would preserve me, and that in times of trial I'd look to him as my refuge. Is there someone you might pray these words for?

Whoever we are, whatever stage of the Christian life we're at, whether circumstances are easy or hard, these are good words to start our day: 'Preserve me, O God, for in you I take refuge.' They remind us of who we are, and they remind us of who God is. On these two truths hang all other Christian teaching and all the Christian life.

2

PSALM 16:2 *Delight*

I say to the L*ORD*, *'You are my Lord;*
I have no good apart from you.'

It's hard to imagine greater words of delight and devotion than these. We can hear the affection in David's voice as he tells God what he means to him; as David also reminds *himself* of what is most precious in life. David knows that where our treasure is, our heart will be also, and so he uses these words to retune his heart, to remind himself of what is most valuable to him: God himself. And David calls us to join in with these words and to retune our hearts as well.

What is the greatest blessing of being a Christian? Is it forgiveness? Is it our guilt and shame taken away? Is it that we have a future hope of heavenly bliss? Is it the prospect of an end of all pain and suffering? Is it the fact that all these things are received by grace alone, not by any good works on our part? There are ten thousand blessings of being a Christian, all of them bright jewels of splendour. But the chief blessing, the jewel in the crown, is Christ himself. It is right that we celebrate all the other blessings, but here David is effectively saying, 'I don't want any of those things unless I also get *God*.'

The bride eyes not her garment
But her dear bridegroom's face

I will not gaze on glory
But on my king of grace
Not on the crown he gives us
But on his nail-pierced hand
The lamb is all the glory
Of Immanuel's land

(Anne Ross Cousin)[2]

—Selah—

In saying, 'I have no good apart from you,' David is not saying that there is nothing of value in the world apart from God himself. It's not honouring to God to say that we don't value anything he has made or anything he gives us. What David reminds himself is that all the good things – both spiritual and physical – are from God himself.

If we try to separate the good things of this world from our Father who gives them, they become idols – and they don't bless us, but enslave us. They taste good at first, but turn to ash in our mouth. Rather, as we receive any good thing, we should – to use C.S. Lewis's wonderful image – trace back up that sunbeam to the sun, God himself.

As believers, we can see the pink and crimson hues of a sunrise as all the more beautiful because they point us to the greater beauty of the Son who will rise in splendour. The taste of good food can point us to the banquet with Christ in the kingdom of God. Every good gift should point us to the God who is good and showers good things on his people.

Knowledge of God helps us rightly enjoy all the things in this world. And enjoyment of all the things of this world rightly can help us in our knowledge of and delight in God.

So today, whatever blessings in the Christian life you celebrate, pray that God would help you to delight in him above all. And whatever good thing in the world you enjoy – and this world is *full* of beauty and wonder – remember to trace back up the sunbeam to God, our chief and our highest good.

3

PSALM 16:3 *Fellowship*

As for the saints in the land, they are the excellent ones,
in whom is all my delight.

When asked what the greatest commandment was, Jesus replied by listing *two* commandments: love God and love neighbour. Loving God with your heart, soul, mind and strength is the most important thing, but this love is always to be accompanied by and expressed in love of neighbour. They can't be separated.

That explains why David speaks as he does in Psalm 16:3. After confessing his devotion to God, David immediately speaks of his delight in God's people. As David looks across the land at all the people, both young and old, rich and poor, native-born or foreigner, he sees only two types of people: those who don't know God, and the 'saints' – God's holy people – who are David's delight.

Life with other Christians isn't always easy. There may be tensions and divisions. We are different in so many ways. Our natural sinful inclinations remain: to be tribal, to form 'inner rings', to neglect those of different social or ethnic backgrounds. We all find it easy to prioritise those who are like us.

Yet, like David, we know something of this delight in other believers. What unites us is greater than what separates us. Dividing walls of hostility are broken down by the gospel.

So ask yourself: when you look at other Christians, what do you see? Do you see the ways in which they are different to you? Do you see your differences in theology? Differences in worship style? Differences in culture and background? Or do you fundamentally see them as 'saints'? These are people who have been made holy by God. These are people for whom Christ shed his precious blood.

—Selah—

In the words of David, we see a glorious pattern of devotion that we as believers are called to follow. But we also see the heart of Jesus Christ, the great king in the line of David. We can hear Psalm 16:3 on his lips. How does Jesus feel about Christians? How does he feel about the church? How does he feel about *you*?

'As for the saints in the land, they are the excellent ones, in whom is all my delight.'

He sees you as holy. He sees you as one of the 'excellent ones'. (Can you hear the pride and affection in his voice...?) You are someone he calls his *delight*.

Not because of our moral goodness. Not because of our perfect theology. Not because of our background or religious credentials. But because he chose to set his affection on us and make us holy. Take comfort in a saviour who delights in you today.

4

PSALM 16:4 *Turning from idols*

The sorrows of those who run after another god shall multiply;
their drink offerings of blood I will not pour out
or take their names on my lips.

David has seen God clearly (vv. 1–2). He knows that God is his refuge, the one who keeps him safe. He knows that there is no good thing apart from the Lord. And he knows the joy of relationship: to be able to say, 'You are *my* God.'

Here we see the necessary flipside of that: David has also seen sin clearly. David's turning *to* God is accompanied by turning *from* false gods. He knows that there is no good apart from the Lord, and so those who run after other gods are sowing the seeds of sorrow and regret.

David resolves not to join in the worship of other gods, or even to take their names on his lips – he wants to be as far away from them as possible. And he urges those around him to share his perspective. We need to remember the sorrow that sin and idolatry causes.

The 'other gods' in view for us may not be the gods of other religions. But these 'gods' are anything we run after for satisfaction, for security, for fulfilment.

Perhaps David speaks from personal experience, remembering how his times of rebellion against the Lord have brought not fulfilment, but misery. We can be so quick to forget the long and tragic history of broken promises that sin has made to us. We can forget that all that looked like the way to freedom turned out to be slavery, all that looked like life turned out to be death, all that promised joy brought ultimately only pain – to us and to others.

Satan's first lie was to tell Adam and Eve that satisfaction could be found *outside* of God and his rules, and that rebellion would carry no consequences. His tactics haven't changed to this day.

—Selah—

Sin has left a devastating wake. Every sorrow, every tear, every cry of anguish is ultimately the result of one of Satan's lies. He came only to kill and destroy. He has no compassion, no empathy. His desire is to increase sorrows, out of sheer hate and spite. David wants to remind himself and others of this; he longs that those around him don't fall into Satan's trap.

Perhaps we are used to thinking of how sin leads to punishment – and of how Christ bore that punishment for us. But dwell also on the *sorrow* that sin causes. Ponder how Christ bore this sorrow as well. No-one knows the damage that sin causes more than Jesus. No-one feels its horror or ugliness more than our saviour. But he tasted these things for us. He became sin for us. He took our sorrows – so that we who have run after other gods may one day be freed from all sorrows, and may have a weight of glory and joy that we can only begin to imagine. He did this so we may gain not just happiness and all the blessings of this world, but God himself.

5

PSALM 16:5–6 *Contentment*

The LORD *is my chosen portion and my cup;*
you hold my lot.
The lines have fallen for me in pleasant places;
indeed, I have a beautiful inheritance.

I'm sure you know the phrase 'The grass is always greener on the other side.' It's the image of looking over your fence at your neighbour's garden and thinking the grass looks greener there.

This phrase has entered our culture to describe the restlessness that we so often know. We look at other people's situations and think their life is better. We are discontent with what we have. This is only made worse by technology, as our capacity to look into other people's lives (perfectly curated and airbrushed, of course) is increased. So much social media involves peering over other people's garden fences, and thinking the grass looks greener there. Life would be better if I could be in *that* situation.

How different this psalm is! When the psalmist says, 'The lines have fallen for me in pleasant places,' he is talking about boundary lines: the allotment of the promised land. Rather than looking and saying, 'The grass looks greener elsewhere,' he's saying, 'I'm happy with what I've been given.'

But are these words only for those in very easy situations? For many of us, our grass is barely green at all: our circumstances are really hard.

David certainly isn't saying we just need to put on a brave face, nor is he pretending that some circumstances aren't really tough. What he is speaking about is more than physical circumstances.

The language here is that of dividing up the promised land, with each family given their 'inheritance'. But what made the land of Israel special was the presence of God with his people. It was the place of relationship, of blessing. God himself is the psalmist's ultimate delight.

This explains how all God's people could join in with this psalm; even someone with a rather barren, rocky field could say, 'The lines have fallen for me in pleasant places.' Better a dry field in the promised land than all the fertile pasturelands of Egypt. To say 'I have a beautiful inheritance' is to look beyond physical circumstances to see spiritual realities. This place I'm in is *good* because it is a place of relationship with the Lord.

—Selah—

We can use the words in this psalm to grow our contentment in the Lord and in his provision. Even if our physical situation is really tough, we can use these words to remember some ultimate realities. If you are a Christian, you live in the kingdom of God, and look forward to the full experience of that reality: the city flowing with the river of life whose architect and builder is God. Whatever our earthly circumstances may be, it is better to be a believer with *this* inheritance!

But if you're anything like me, you'll find yourself prone to envy people not just in the world around us, but within the church as well. I can so easily envy the situations other Christians find themselves in. At such times, Psalm 16 reminds me of all I have in the Lord – of my beautiful inheritance.

How can I envy my brother or sister? Do they have more of God than I do? Has Christ shed more blood for them than for me? Is my salvation any less complete than theirs? Are the royal robes I wear any less glorious? Are they heading to any greater city? Will they gaze upon a more lovely saviour?

6

PSALM 16:7–8 *Security*

I bless the Lord *who gives me counsel;*
in the night also my heart instructs me.
I have set the Lord *always before me;*
because he is at my right hand, I shall not be shaken.

We all long for stability. The confidence to know that we will not be shaken, no matter what comes. But many of us feel that such stability and assuredness is beyond our reach.

David's confidence to face the day ahead comes not from within, but from the presence of the Lord with him. And so he sets his eyes on God. Part of David's stability comes from the Lord giving David counsel. God directs David, leads him, guides him: his word is a lamp to his feet.

God's commands are not burdensome to David – because he knows who God is. God is good, and so leads his people in good paths – the paths of *life*, as this psalm will go on to say. God's counsel to David is part of his personal, purposeful care for him.

That's why David moves so freely from speaking of God's word *to* him to speaking of God's presence *with* him in the next verse: 'he is at my right hand'. God speaks to make himself *present* to his people. God speaks to create and to sustain relationship with his people. So even 'in the night' – perhaps when David cannot sleep – his heart is instructed as he meditates on God's word which he has hidden in his heart.

As David hears the voice of God in the Scriptures, he knows the delightful presence of his Lord to comfort and guide him. And the same is true for us today.

—Selah—

'I have set the LORD always before me.' David is deliberate here, he is intentional. God cannot be seen by any human eye, but with the eyes of faith David sets the Lord before him. David binds and restrains his thoughts from running elsewhere, and directs them to the Lord.

Often our circumstances are beyond our capacity to change. But David knows that we can choose what we set our gaze upon. Rather than let his heart be tossed and turned towards earthly temptations or human worries, David fixes his gaze on the Lord.

The Lord is at his right hand – like a staff to lean on when the road is rocky. It is the Lord David looks to, whatever life throws at him. The result of this: David will never be shaken. There is a stability and confidence to those who set the Lord before them as their hope and refuge. There is great comfort in deliberately pondering the support the Lord gives, and his presence with us in distress. David wants us to know, and to share in, the unshakeable security of those who set their hearts on God.

Place before your heart the lamb whose blood was shed for you.

Fill your thoughts with the one who was raised to life.

Fix your eyes on the one who now lives to intercede for you.

What griefs we needlessly suffer because we don't fill our hearts with *this* saviour! Could we ever spend too much time in contemplation of *this* Lord?

7

PSALM 16:9–10 *Hope*

Therefore my heart is glad, and my whole being rejoices;
my flesh also dwells secure.
For you will not abandon my soul to Sheol,
or let your holy one see corruption.

Gladness. Joy. Confidence. This psalm builds to a joyous crescendo as it ends – but what causes David to feel like this?

What has been hinted at so far in the psalm now becomes explicit: the hope of resurrection. Resurrection makes sense of all David has said so far: giving perspective on this life, and giving solid hope for the future.

David and other Old Testament saints did not have the full picture of resurrection that we know from the New Testament. But even so, there was a growing hope of life after death. To put it bluntly, God's promises were too big and weighty to be completely fulfilled in this life. In this life, there is always a gap between God's promise and the full experience of the reality.

Could the God of this psalm abandon his faithful people to the grave (Sheol)? Could he be a refuge only for this life? Could he be the chief good if he was powerless against the greatest enemy? Would our Lord really be any better than other gods if he was just as impotent as them against death? Would God's promises be worth trusting if they had an end date: the day we lie in the grave?

Because of what he knows of God's character, David rejoices and dwells secure. God's promises are so great that they must overflow from this life into eternity. A God of this much goodness and life *must* be a God who keeps his people beyond the grave.

—Selah—

Perhaps Jesus meditated on this psalm as he approached his death. Perhaps these were the promises that helped him to fix his eyes on the resurrection joy set before him, and so endure the cross, scorning its shame.

In Acts 2, Peter sees this psalm as pointing to the resurrection of Jesus. Christ suffered for our sins and tasted death for us, but the Lord did not abandon him to the grave, instead raised him to the place of all honour. Jesus saw the light of life and was satisfied.

This is why we can fully know the hope of resurrection that David only began to see. Christ is the firstfruits. His resurrection guarantees ours. In fact, because believers are united to him, Christ's resurrection *is* our resurrection! We are tightly bound to Christ, hidden in him. Our fate is now irrevocably tied to his.

Just ponder what that means for a moment. My flesh dwells secure, because my life is hid in Christ and he now dwells in security in the palace of heaven.

God will not abandon me to the grave, because Christ entered the grave and plundered its captives, so death has power no longer.

And so, hidden in Christ, my heart is glad, my whole being rejoices. How secure is my position? How certain is my future? As sure and certain as that of Christ himself.

8

PSALM 16:11 *Joy*

You make known to me the path of life;
in your presence there is fullness of joy;
at your right hand are pleasures for evermore.

Have you ever heard Christianity described as joyless, life-denying or boring? That's a common portrayal these days. Anyone who thinks of the Christian faith as dry, dull or restrictive needs to read and meditate on Psalm 16 again. Look at the words used: 'life'; 'fullness of joy'; 'pleasures for evermore'. The Christian faith is one of joy and delight and life, because this is what God is like.

Our path is one that leads to life. Wherever we are, whatever situation we're in, this morning we woke up one day closer to fullness of life in the presence of God; to the life that is true life. This is not just existence beyond the grave, but a whole different quality of life – sharing in the life of God himself.

We will have fullness of joy in God's presence. Our God is a joyful God. He is the happiest being in the universe. His joy is overflowing, infectious, life-giving, wilderness-transforming. As Jesus said to his disciples, he wants his joy to be in them, and their joy to be complete. God is joyful, and he wants his people to share in that joy.

Even in this world, stained with sin and sorrow, we can know joy and pleasure. The bustle and laughter of a sunny afternoon at the park;

staying up late to talk with loved ones; that cake that tastes twice as good because Grandma just brought it round; the stand erupting as your team wins promotion to the Premier League; the unexpected kindness of a stranger; the long-awaited visit of a friend.

If God can fill even *this* world with such pleasures, then imagine what he's preparing in his own country. If God can make appetisers like these, then imagine when the banquet itself begins.

We will have 'pleasures for evermore' at God's 'right hand'. Can we even begin to imagine what this will be like? What the God of wonder and mirth will have prepared for those who love him?

—Selah—

With such a destination in view, surely our Christian life can be called 'the path of life'. But there is also life *now*. What makes our destination so delightful is not the streets of gold so much as the presence of God himself. He is the chief joy – the fountain from which every other blessing springs.

We know the joy of his presence *now*, even as we journey. He has sent his Spirit into our hearts, the same Spirit that filled Jesus with joy when he walked this earth (Luke 10:21).

Jesus came so that we may have life to the full: an entering into the joyous, rich fellowship of Father, Son and Spirit. The greatest, most passionate celebration the world has ever known.

Our God will spend an eternity delighting to do good to us, showing us the immeasurable riches of his grace, calling us to drink deeper of his love and the eternal pleasures at his right hand.

Life. Fullness of joy. Pleasures for evermore. These are the blessings of being in relationship with *this* God – the God who *is* life and joy and pleasure.

9

PSALM 27:1 *The Lord is my light*

The Lord *is my light and my salvation;*
whom shall I fear?
The Lord *is the stronghold of my life;*
of whom shall I be afraid?

Psalm 27 could hardly begin with three stronger images: light, salvation, stronghold. The rest of the psalm will reveal a situation of great distress – enemies who pour out violence, evildoers who seek to devour David. Yet they are not given the first word. David begins by reminding himself – and others who join in singing this psalm – who God is. Today we'll look just at the first of these images: the Lord is my *light*.

Light to guide us. For David, in distress and on the run, light is what he needs to guide him. Perhaps you've had the experience of being lost, trying to find your way in the dark. We stumble, we take the wrong path. But then light begins to dawn, and we can see the way to go.

The Lord is David's light, the one who leads him and helps him see – like the Israelites in the wilderness were led by the Lord's pillar of cloud and fire. Maybe for you, things seem dark, the way seems unclear, and there seems to be no safe path to walk. In times like these, David would encourage us with the fact that the Lord is our light.

Light that brings life. As well as guiding us, light is associated with *life* (John 8:12). Each spring, trees and flowers begin to sprout and grow as the sun comes out. As plants drink in the rays of the sun, they blossom and bear fruit. In the same way, the Lord is the one who gives life to all things. He makes us grow, blossom and flourish. God is the source of all goodness and beauty.

—Selah—

Light that overcomes darkness. Perhaps chief among the uses of the light images in Scripture is light overcoming darkness. Darkness is a powerful symbol of evil, threat and uncertainty. We live in a dark world. We live in a world where evil people do evil deeds. Perhaps we even fear walking through our own town or city while it is dark, for fear of what might befall us.

Yet in a dark world, the Lord is light. Light that exposes the deeds of wickedness. Light that drives away darkness and evil. David faces darkness: evil, threats, enemies. But the Lord is his light who conquers all of these, and keeps David safe.

We see these things most clearly in Jesus Christ, the light of the world. For a little while it looked as if darkness had the upper hand. As Christ hung on the cross, the whole sky went dark at midday. Darkness did its worst, but as dawn broke on that first Easter Day, the light of the new creation broke through, never again to be dimmed.

Christ is the light who guides us, who brings life and every other blessing, and who shines even in the darkness. And so we look to him, knowing the darkness has been defeated, knowing that the new day is dawning. We look to him, awaiting the final glorious sunrise of the Son of God in radiant glory, when we shall say with ever-increasing joy, 'The Lord is my light'!

10

PSALM 27:1
My salvation and stronghold

The L*ORD* *is my light and my salvation;*
whom shall I fear?
The L*ORD* *is the stronghold of my life;*
of whom shall I be afraid?

In the last devotion, we looked at the first of three strong images that begin this psalm. Together they make a threefold cord of security that is not easily broken. Here we consider the second and third images: the Lord is my salvation, and the Lord is my stronghold.

When surrounded by enemies, David knows that his confidence is not in his own strength, his wealth or his wisdom. The *Lord* will save him. The Lord is his stronghold.

The picture here is of a rocky crag in the Judean wilderness – a place of protection from enemies. A place of solid and enduring rock under and around you. As your fingers trace the rough surface and the weathering of centuries, you remember that here the outcome won't be determined by pure numbers or by the hostility of the enemy. It is a place of safety.

The Lord is like this rocky stronghold and so David won't be afraid. Not because his situation is easy, but because the Lord is mighty. Evildoers are intent on doing David harm. They are pictured as devouring beasts, surrounding David. But David is in a place of security: the Lord is his stronghold and salvation.

This was something David needed to see by faith. Most of the time he was not secure in a rocky stronghold, safe from his enemies. Often his circumstances were very uncertain, and he felt very weak and vulnerable. But David knew that though he was weak, the *Lord* was his stronghold.

David teaches us to look beyond our circumstances – which often we cannot change – to greater realities about who God is. Trace your fingers over the rough and enduring rock of the character and promises of God. Feel the ancient walls around. David's security was not bound up in the ups and downs of his life, but in the God who held him safe in his grip. And the same is true for us today.

—Selah—

But notice that David doesn't simply say that God saves him. He says more than that: God *is* his salvation. Salvation is more than rescue from danger – whether the literal enemies David faced, or our greater enemies of sin and death. Of course, this is part of it, but the greatest part of our salvation is being in relationship with God. Being with God, knowing him personally, this is the heart of salvation. The greatest gift God gives to us is *himself*.

The Lord is my light. The Lord is my salvation. The Lord is my stronghold. These truths are the bedrock on which we stand. Why not make these a prayer you repeat regularly. Why not pray them for those you know and love who are in distress: Lord, be their light, their salvation and their stronghold. We can exercise delightful dependence on our Lord by praying for the very things he has promised, knowing that these are prayers he loves to hear and answer:

Lord, this world is dark – be my light.
Lord, my trials are great – be my salvation.
Lord, I don't feel strong – be the stronghold of my life.

11

PSALM 27:2–3
Though enemies attack

When evildoers assail me
to eat up my flesh,
my adversaries and foes,
it is they who stumble and fall.
Though an army encamp against me,
my heart shall not fear;
though war arise against me,
yet I will be confident.

Life can be really hard as a Christian. There are all the usual struggles of life in a broken and fractured world, but also the opposition and hostility we can face for our faith. We've received extraordinary promises from God, but life in the day-to-day can feel very far from this. It's one of the reasons I love the psalms; they are so honest about what we go through as believers.

David himself was a man of many trials. He describes enemies attacking him, using the imagery of wild beasts who seek to eat up his flesh and armies encamped against him. For David, the enemies were often literal enemies, coming against him with sword and spear. But ultimately they were the enemies that are introduced at the beginning of the book of Psalms in Psalm 2: those who oppose God. As God's chosen king, David felt the particular force of that, but as God's people, we face that opposition too.

For many Christians today, the enemies are just as physical as in David's day. Believers all round the world face the threat of physical violence and persecution just because they worship Jesus. Psalm 27 gives us words we can pray in solidarity with persecuted believers: praying that God would protect them against enemies, and help them not to fear. For those of us whose situations are more comfortable, Psalm 27 can expand our horizon to bring to mind suffering brothers and sisters around the world, and help us to empathise with them and pray for them.

—Selah—

But even if not all of us face literal enemies, all God's people have an enemy in Satan, who prowls around like a roaring lion looking for someone to devour. Satan uses the hardships of this world to try to unsettle us and undermine our faith. Life in this world is *hard*.

Yet even in the midst of enemies, David says he can be confident. He is applying the truths that God is his light, salvation and stronghold. David knows that even when enemies attack, it is they – not him – who stumble and fall. David does not fear, because he knows the enemies will not ultimately prevail.

This is most clearly seen in the cross of Christ. When enemies came against Jesus, seeking to devour him, they stumbled. The cross looked like Satan's victory, but it was his downfall. And the cross is the lens through which we must view all other suffering, all other enemies.

Those who oppose us seem strong, but they ultimately stumble and fall. When Satan wounds us, even though that may be almost unbearably painful, this is no victory for him. Somehow – and we wish sometimes we could *see* how – God uses even Satan's worst attacks to do us good. When Satan sends trials, which may make us despair of ever seeing the light, God does not allow them to shipwreck us, but rather uses these to refine our faith. Even Satan's greatest weapon, death, is no longer to be feared, as it is now a means of ushering us into the glorious presence of our God, and into the welcoming arms of our saviour.

12

PSALM 27:4 *One thing I ask*

One thing have I asked of the Lord,
that will I seek after:
that I may dwell in the house of the Lord
all the days of my life,
to gaze upon the beauty of the Lord
and to enquire in his temple.

Our desires reveal a lot about us. If I were asked what one thing I most desire, I'm sure that I would answer with something noble like 'world peace' or some spiritual equivalent. But, of course, our desires are revealed in the decisions we take, the things we pursue day-to-day. Being less busy. Being more financially secure. Improving a certain relationship. Progressing in my career. Getting out of a mess. Sometimes it's as simple as football on the TV and a comfy chair to sit in.

David says his one desire – the one thing he asks for – is that he may dwell in the house of the Lord and see God. David's eyes are not on the enemies surrounding him, nor on the trials he is facing. His one request of God is not for deliverance – as surely might be natural in his situation of distress. But his focus is what he is being delivered *for*: dwelling with God.

David wants to dwell in the 'house of the Lord', meaning the 'temple' (or before it, the 'tabernacle') where God dwelt among his people. David's desire is for God himself. David doesn't see God simply as a vending machine who gives protection, provision and salvation. David knows that our hearts were made for more even than forgiveness, eternal life and the thousand other blessings of the gospel. We were made for God – and so David wants to gaze on *him*.

—Selah—

The reason David wants to be in the house of God is seen in the second half of verse 4: 'to gaze upon the beauty of the LORD'. David treasures God above all other things. For him, there is no greater joy or treasure than gazing on the beauty of his Lord, pondering his wonderful character and goodness. Do we often think of the Lord as *beautiful*? Do we ponder the beauty of his character? David finds his Lord utterly captivating. He doesn't just want to glance at the Lord's beauty, he wants to *gaze*.

There is a virtuous circle here that David invites us into. Only when we spend time gazing on the Lord do we see his overwhelming beauty – which in turn increases our affection for him, and our desire to spend time with him. And so it continues.

David wants to help us reorient our desire and redirect our love. These words are not to condemn us, but for us to join in with and grow into: a liturgy that retunes our hearts.

Gaze on Christ in the Scriptures. Encounter him in public worship. Seek to commune with him daily. And long for the day when we'll gaze on the beautiful facc of our saviour as he welcomes us to glory.

13

PSALM 27:5 *He will hide me*

For he will hide me in his shelter
in the day of trouble;
he will conceal me under the cover of his tent;
he will lift me high upon a rock.

The 'day of trouble'. That day that we fear. The day when our worst fears come true, and we feel powerless. For all of us, there is a day and a circumstance that feels beyond us. Up to this point, we might be able to cope, but if *that* should happen... We dare not even think about it.

It is in *that* day that we receive the greatest provision from the Lord. In *that* day, 'he will hide me in his shelter'. He will 'conceal me under the cover of his tent'. He will 'lift me high upon a rock'.

In the day when we want to curl up and hide, God steps in and hides us. In the day when we want to pull the blankets over our head and escape from the frightening world, God lays *his* blanket of protection over us. In the day when we just want to run far away, God lifts us. He lifts us onto a high rock, where we are safe from our enemies. This doesn't always mean we are removed *from* the day of trouble, but we are kept safe *in* the day of trouble. He brings us to a place of safety. He lifts us into the arms of Christ, the rock of our salvation.

He hides *me*. He covers *me*. He lifts *me*. When days of extraordinary trial come, God answers them with extraordinary provision and tenderness. There is might here, but also great personal care. This is what it means for God to be our light, our salvation, our stronghold.

—Selah—

These are precious images to meditate on. They are promises to push deep into our souls. But any promise of God can also become words we pray back to him – after all, prayer is always asking for what God has promised to give. So we can lay hold of these promises as we pray them back to God – and perhaps for some of us, these are words we need today:

Lord, hide me in your shelter in this day of trouble
Father, conceal me under the cover of your tent. May I find peace and security in your presence.
Lord Jesus, lift me high into you, my rock and my place of safety.

—Selah—

These are also words we could pray for other people – perhaps for a family member or a loved one who is facing a day of trouble. So often we don't know what to pray. So often we fail to pray because our words feel tired and repetitive. But here are words to pray earnestly for our fellow believers – knowing that as God has promised these very things, our prayers will never be in vain:

Lord, for my friend who is experiencing a day of trouble…
Hide her in your shelter.
Conceal her under the cover of your tent.
Lift her high on a rock.

And even as we pray, we do so with confidence, knowing that these prayers will be answered – *have* been answered – in Christ, our rock and our redeemer.

14

PSALM 27:6
My head shall be lifted

And now my head shall be lifted up
above my enemies all round me,
and I will offer in his tent
sacrifices with shouts of joy;
I will sing and make melody to the Lord.

This verse expresses astonishing confidence. David is still surrounded by enemies, and if you look on in the psalm, you'll see there are anguished prayers of lament to come. Yet even in this situation, he has his eyes on the future. The enemies will not have the final word. David's painful circumstances will not win the day. His head will not be bowed in defeat, but be lifted up in triumph.

David knows that God has got hold of his people and will not let them go. David knows that no-one can snatch any of God's people from his hand. Not only is David sure of victory, but also of vindication. His head will be lifted above his enemies.

We're reminded of Psalm 23, where the Lord prepares a banquet for his beloved, even in the face of enemies. This is no quiet escape from peril, but a public and triumphant celebration. The Lord wants the world to know that his people are loved, and secure. We are like the prodigal son, embraced by his father *outside* the house in full view of the neighbours, because the father wants everyone to know that this son is *loved* and is welcomed home.

Suffering, you do not have the victory! Addiction, you will not ultimately triumph! Pain, your reign of terror will soon be ended! Guilt, those last vestiges of power you try to hold over even those who are forgiven, these will be broken! Besetting sin, you will no longer lurk just out of sight, ready to pounce, but you will be banished forever! Sadness, you will cast your cold shadow no longer! Death, you are the last enemy to be defeated, and your defeat is sure!

—Selah—

History is heading in one direction, and one only. We are moving towards the day when we will join in endless song to our Lord. We will offer sacrifices – not sacrifices for sin, but joyful sacrifices of praise and thanksgiving for what God has done. David looks forward to celebrating with God's people, telling stories of his grace. He looks forward to singing and making melody to the Lord in his house of wine and song. And he knows this outcome is assured. This is what it means for God to be his light, his salvation, his stronghold.

How much more as Christians can we share this confidence. Jesus Christ has already had his head lifted up above his enemies. He has conquered the grave, he has put Satan to open shame, he has disarmed the powers and principalities, and he has won the victory. He has won *our* victory, because we are united to him; his story is our story.

We enjoy this victory in part now, but fully and finally on the day we are lifted to glory. Then we will be lifted up above our enemies, and presented before the watching world as bright trophies of God's grace. And the song of praise we've begun on earth will erupt into a glorious symphony, and we will sing and make melody to our precious Lord forever.

These are the truths that keep us going. These are the truths that keep us singing.

15

PSALM 27:7–8
Seeking God's face

Hear, O Lord, when I cry aloud;
be gracious to me and answer me!
You have said, 'Seek my face.'
My heart says to you,
'Your face, Lord, do I seek.'

Our Christian journey is like a journey through a mountain range. Even as we are slowly ascending higher and higher towards the summit, there are valleys along the way. The beginning of Psalm 27 was a 'high ground' experience of joy and peace in God. But in verse 7, the mood changes dramatically. The psalmist is back in the valley. Maybe that sort of change reflects what we've gone through in our own Christian lives. If so, maybe we've wondered what to make of this. Do cries of anguish like we find here really belong with the words of trust found earlier in the psalm?

But in Psalm 27, David pours out his heart like this *because* of what he believes about God. Loud prayers, anguished tears, cries for God to *do* something – these are cries of faith. These are cries that come from a heart that believes deep down – however much present experience seems to contradict this – that God is light, salvation and stronghold.

David's real faith leads to real honesty. There is urgency and intensity to how David prays: 'Hear', 'be gracious', and 'answer'. This is no casual prayer. For David, it is life and death. He is wrestling with God, just as Jacob did. He is making his prayers with loud cries and tears to God, just as our saviour would do. And he encourages us to do the same.

—Selah—

Even in times of distress, David's greatest desire is to seek God's face. He wants intimacy with God and access to his presence. He desires closeness and an unhindered relationship. This is an echo of what he has said previously: his one desire is to gaze upon the beauty of the Lord and to seek him in his temple. David longs to be close to God and to see his Fatherly smile.

Isn't that something that so many of us want, deep down? We may be preoccupied with so many other things, but when we stop and think, what so many of us long for is this warm intimacy with God. But is it possible?

The command 'Seek my face' is plural – addressed to all God's people. It is both command and invitation. The Lord calls us to seek him, because he wants to be found. He calls us to come to him, because he wants communion with us. He calls us to love him, because he wants to bestow his own love on us. When Christ died on the cross, he was stretching wide his arms of invitation to his people. *Seek me! Come to me! Find rest in me!*

In our times of trial, we can pour out our hearts with tumbling phrases, calling on God to answer. Often we can do no better than David's words here: 'be gracious to me and answer me!'

We do this because he's asked us to. He's called us and enabled us to seek him. But he's not even waited for us to make the first move. Even before we seek him, he came to seek us.

16

PSALM 27:9–10
Do not forsake me

Hide not your face from me.
Turn not your servant away in anger,
O you who have been my help.
Cast me not off; forsake me not,
O God of my salvation!
For my father and my mother have forsaken me,
but the Lord *will take me in.*

'My father and my mother have forsaken me.' As you read these words, somewhere around the world, Christian believers will be facing persecution from their own family because of their faith. For some, it is being cast out of the family; for some, it is the threat of violence or death. Simply because they turned to Christ and turned away from their family's religion.

Mercifully, many of us do not face such physical persecution. But rejection – especially from family members – doesn't need to be physical, doesn't even need to be spoken at all, to be very real and very painful. Perhaps we experience a coldness and distance. Perhaps it spills over into anger at our views on sexuality. Perhaps we are told in a hundred unspoken ways that we do not fit, or are not welcome.

Facing this rejection from family, David calls on the Lord to act differently. The psalm began by addressing the 'LORD' – God's covenant name, and the verses here are saturated with covenant terms: 'your servant'; do not 'forsake' me. When David experiences the pain of broken relationship with family, he appeals to the God of covenant, of committed faithful relationship.

God's covenant promises mean that David prays all these things *confident* of an answer, beautifully expressed in the final verse of our section: 'the LORD will take me in'.

—Selah—

These are words we can pray with even greater confidence this side of the cross of Christ.

The Lord has not hidden his face from us, but in Christ his face has turned ever towards us in blessing.

The Lord will not turn us away in anger, because on the cross Christ was turned away in anger so we could be welcomed in love.

The Lord will not cast us off or forsake us because Christ is now risen and seated with God in the place of highest honour – and we are united to him, with our future as secure as his.

When we don't feel at home in the world, we know we always have a home in God. A place of peace and security.

So like David, we can cry out to God, 'Do not forsake me.' We can pray these verses in solidarity with brothers and sisters around the world who may be facing violence and persecution today.

But we can also thank God that these prayers have been answered in Christ. Even in this life, we have extraordinary access to the throne of grace, and a home among his people – a new family. And we look forward to the day when in the fullest and richest sense 'the LORD will take me in'. When he will greet us at gates of gold and welcome us into eternal dwellings.

17

PSALM 27:11 *Teach me your way*

Teach me your way, O Lord,
and lead me on a level path
because of my enemies.

We must beware a tendency to think that the Christian life is primarily about knowing the right things, that we just need to really understand the gospel and we'll be ok.

The Scriptures consistently call us to walk in God's ways. Right thinking is essential, but it is not the sum of the Christian life. Jesus calls his followers to 'believe in me', but he also calls them to 'follow me'.

David wants to walk in God's ways – to pursue the moral virtues that God desires in his people. The second line of this verse continues this idea; the 'level path' is not so much about comfort, but has a moral sense: it could be translated 'upright paths'. David isn't looking for the easy road, he is wanting to walk in holiness.

This is a prayer for all circumstances. It would be a good way for us to start each day: 'Teach me your way, O Lord, and lead me on a level path.' And we can pray the same thing for other people as well – perhaps family members:

'Lord, teach my grandchildren your way today, and lead them on a level path.'

We don't know what the day may hold, but we can pray that in our decisions we would seek God's way, and we would pursue level paths of holiness.

If the Christian life is a path, we might also ask what habits and patterns will help us as we walk. At times, I think I've been so afraid of legalism that I've not cultivated healthy habits and practices; I've minimised this aspect of the Christian life as a 'walk'. What habits could you cultivate to help you walk in God's paths? What habits might help you increasingly 'gaze upon the beauty of the LORD'?

—*Selah*—

Did you notice here that David prays to be led in upright paths *because of* his enemies. David prays these things while still being surrounded by enemies, wild beasts who would do him harm. We might expect David to ask God to lead him in paths of escape, rather than paths of righteousness. We might expect David even to turn to illicit paths. But David pursues God. He realises that more than ever he needs to walk God's way.

I can so often think that walking in God's ways is something for when times are easy. When life calms down a bit, I'll start praying more, I'll devote myself to reading the Bible, I'll pursue holiness. Maybe I think that these are optional extras, only for when life is under control.

No matter how limited our choices and options may be, *the Lord's way* is always open to us. What an encouragement this is. The Lord is far more concerned with us seeking him, and seeking his way, than the actual circumstances we find ourselves in. We don't need to wish we were in a different situation, where we could serve the Lord better. Every day we can pray, 'teach me your paths', and seek to honour God where we are.

18

PSALM 27:12 *False witnesses*

Give me not up to the will of my adversaries;
for false witnesses have risen against me,
and they breathe out violence.

Our society is one where there is opposition to the claims of Jesus and the lifestyle of his followers. Christians are often misunderstood and misrepresented. It is incredibly hard when people say things about us that are not true; when people make false accusations. Words carry great power; characters can be ruined and great emotional damage done by false witnesses who speak untrue words.

When we read the Scriptures, we see that this is nothing new. God's people have always faced hostility from those who hate him. David models how we can cry out to God in such times, and entrust ourselves to him who judges justly. These are also words we can cry out on behalf of Christian brothers and sisters who face such false accusations.

But, of course, it's hard for us to read these words about 'false witnesses' and not think of Jesus Christ, who most fully experienced what is described here.

Jesus lived the perfect life of a believer. He lived all of Psalm 27. He knew false witnesses rising against him. He was surrounded by men breathing out violence, ultimately taking him to the cross. Yet through all this he did not return evil for evil, but entrusted himself to God; he always took the Lord's way, he always followed the upright path.

Here – as indeed in all the sufferings of the psalmists – we gain an insight into the heart of Christ himself. In the psalms, perhaps in a way that we don't get elsewhere in Scripture, we see so clearly what Christ went through described from the inside. We learn something of what it *felt* like. In the anguished words of David and the psalmists, we can hear the heart-cries of our saviour. What a perspective this gives us on the cross. What a window into what it cost Christ to achieve our salvation. Take a moment now to worship Christ for what he went through, for *you*.

—Selah—

But what confidence this gives us as *we* pray Psalm 27. We pray knowing that one has lived this way before us. What comfort to know that we are not alone when we are opposed and maligned. What comfort to know that these things are not a sign of failure in the Christian life, but a sign that we belong to Christ. The worst that the world can say about us – and we must never minimise the pain of this – in fact only proclaims all the more loudly that we belong to Christ!

What hope there is as we know that Christ's anguished cries were heard by the Lord. The adversaries did not triumph. Satan – *the* accuser, *the* false witness – does not have the final word. Christ was raised and vindicated for the world to see. Instead of shame and dishonour, he received a double portion, and everlasting joy (Is. 61:7). And, as those united to him, this is our story, this is our future.

19

PSALM 27:13
The goodness of the Lord

I believe that I shall look upon the goodness of the Lord
in the land of the living!

The psalm finishes as it began, with rich confidence in God. David is still facing trials, he is still surrounded by enemies like ravenous beasts. But David believes he will see 'the goodness of the Lord in the land of the living' – which in the psalms refers to *this life*, not to a hope beyond the grave.

David's confidence is not based on circumstances, but on the character of God. This is the place where his meditation in the rest of the psalm has brought him. David meditated on the greatness of the Lord (vv. 1–3), he longed to gaze upon the beauty of the Lord (vv. 4–5), now he is sure he will look upon the goodness of the Lord. And David wants us to share his confidence. We too should say, 'I believe that I shall look upon the goodness of the Lord in the land of the living!'

Expect to see the Lord's goodness today. Anticipate his grace and tender mercy. Look forward to experiencing his favour and smile upon you. Like David, our circumstances may be hard, but we should still expect to look upon the Lord's goodness in the land of the living.

Sometimes we need to lift our eyes to see these things. We need to pray that the Lord would help us to see his goodness. J.I. Packer puts it this way in his book *Knowing God*:

Appreciate the goodness of God. Count your blessings. Learn not to take natural benefits, endowments, and pleasures for granted; learn to thank God for them all... every meal, every pleasure, every possession, every bit of sun, every night's sleep, every moment of health and safety, everything else that sustains and enriches life, is a divine gift. And how abundant these gifts are![3]

Oh how abundant indeed! Psalm 27:13 provides words to set as the background music of our lives: 'I shall look upon the goodness of the LORD in the land of the living!' These are words to turn into prayer: 'Lord, open my eyes to see your goodness today.' These are words to pray for our loved ones: 'Lord, even in this time of trial, may they see your goodness and grace.'

—Selah—

David had plenty of reasons to believe he'd see the Lord's goodness. He saw the Lord's goodness in the sacrificial system, in the Lord's acts of deliverance, in his daily provision. But we have seen the Lord's goodness in the face of Christ.

If David could be sure of the Lord's goodness even before the cross, how much deeper do we know the goodness of the one who did not withhold his own son. If you have doubts about the Lord's goodness, bring them to the cross. If you have questions about the Lord's plans for us, bring them to the cross. See the goodness of Jesus shown in iron nails and bloody hands.

Whatever the next few weeks and months of our lives may hold, God *will* show us his goodness. We'll know life, breath and a thousand other blessings, all of them tokens of a God who will never stop doing us good. Every day we can see his goodness, because every day he'll give us *himself*.

Let today be a day in which you actively seek to see the Lord's goodness. Gaze on his glorious character. Look for evidences of his grace. Cultivate a wonder at the generosity and goodness of the Lord.

20

PSALM 27:14 *Wait for the Lord*

Wait for the Lord;
be strong, and let your heart take courage;
wait for the Lord!

As the psalm closes, David is still awaiting full deliverance. He does not fully experience all the blessings that will one day be his. He has not yet gazed face to face on the beauty of the Lord, or fully experienced his goodness. And so he waits. As commentator Derek Kidner puts it, he is holding on in 'naked faith'.[4]

Perhaps we know this feeling. We battle with seemingly unanswered prayers. Our circumstances seem to contradict the very truths about God that Psalm 27 celebrates. The wait is long – too long, it seems.

David tells us to wait, but not passively or as if the future is uncertain. We are to wait in expectation, in certain hope. David trusts in the Lord's goodness, and so he submits to the Lord's timing (which, let's be honest, is not always what David would want or what we would want).

The default posture of the Christian life is that of waiting. We live in the gap between promise and reality. We don't yet fully experience all the blessings and riches we have in Christ – not until Christ returns. And so we wait. We live in hope – a hope that is certain and sure. We long for Christ's appearing (2 Tim. 4:8).

—Selah—

This waiting can be hard; long periods of God's seeming delay can be discouraging and cause fears to rise. So David urges us to 'be strong, and let your heart take courage'. But how can those who are weak be told to 'be strong'? How can the fearful simply be told to 'take courage'?

David is not calling us to look within ourselves, but rather to do what he did when facing severe trial: 'David strengthened himself in the LORD his God' (1 Sam. 30:6). The strength we need is the strength of our God who is light and salvation and stronghold. When we have no strength to face the day – and if we're self-aware, we'll realise that this is the case every day – we rest in the one who is strong for us.

This is the way Christ lived. He did not sail through life without cares or difficulties. He was not 'strong' in a worldly sense. He was a man of sorrows and infirmities. How we need to rid ourselves of the idea that Christians are those with no struggles. That Christians must be sorted people, who conform to middle-class expectations of health, wealth or strength. Christ had none of these. But he strengthened himself in God. He waited for the Lord. He too lived by 'naked faith'.

And Christ now says to us, 'Wait for the LORD.' These are his words to you today. This is his *prayer* for you today. That you find your hope and strength in God. That you prove God to be a loving and compassionate Father, just as Christ himself did. Hear these words on the lips of Christ, expressing his heart for you today: 'be strong, and let your heart take courage; wait for the LORD!'

21

PSALM 34:1–3
Bless the Lord at all times

Of David, when he changed his behaviour before Abimelech, so that he drove him out, and he went away.

I will bless the Lord *at all times;*
his praise shall continually be in my mouth.
My soul makes its boast in the Lord*;*
let the humble hear and be glad.
Oh, magnify the Lord *with me,*
and let us exalt his name together!

As this psalm begins, we find David on the run, as he so often was. The heading at the top of this psalm locates it when David had been driven out by the Philistine king Abimelech. The narrative in the book of Samuel tells us that David went to hide in the cave of Adullam, where there gathered to him all who were in distress, in debt and bitter in soul (1 Sam. 22:1–2). David had been anointed king of Israel, but now found himself far from Jerusalem and far from the throne. Things were bleak. Yet in this situation of distress, David can say, 'I will bless the Lord at all times.' Even in the desert, he worships.

Perhaps we've known the beauty of songs rising from the lips of suffering believers. For all the splendour of this world – towering mountains, meadows crowded with spring flowers – none of these match the beauty of God's people who choose to praise him even in the face of great hardship. How precious in the ears of the Lord are the songs of his suffering saints!

Psalm 34 is deeply personal testimony: 'I sought the LORD, and he answered me.' But David calls those around him to join in with him: 'Oh, magnify the LORD with me, and let us exalt his name together!'

The secret to David's praise is that he magnifies the Lord – David continually increases his own vision of God. David's eyes are not on the cave walls around him, but on the God who overshadows him in love. And David calls on all those who are in distress and bitter in soul to look up. Look at the greatness of the Lord! Make your boast in the Lord! This is why even the 'humble' – which could mean 'afflicted' – can be glad. David isn't minimising his circumstances, he is magnifying God.

—Selah—

Hundreds of years after David, another anointed king found himself far from the throne in Jerusalem, persecuted and marginalised. But Jesus kept praising God. He too kept trusting his Father. And he too sets an example for his people to follow. Like David, Jesus wisely pastors his people, and leads them in devotion to God. Hear Jesus' voice to you today, from the very throne room of heaven: 'Oh, magnify the LORD with mc, and lct us exalt his name together!'

Will we join with our king and brother? Will we join in praise to God – even in the desert – looking forward to the day when we'll join with the angels, with countless multitudes and with all creation in praising our Lord forever?

Magnify the Lord. Bless the Lord at all times and in all situations. Let his praise be continually in your mouth. And if you still don't feel like doing this, read on, as the rest of the psalm will pile up reasons why God is worthy of such ceaseless praise.

22

PSALM 34:4–5 *He answered me*

I sought the Lord, and he answered me
and delivered me from all my fears.
Those who look to him are radiant,
and their faces shall never be ashamed.

'I sought the Lord and he answered me.' This is the foundation for the rest of this psalm, the immovable granite bedrock on which everything else stands firm. This is what enables David to say he will bless the Lord at all times and in all situations. This is what leads to David's words of encouragement to all those with him.

Whatever else may be going on, whatever circumstances David is in, David knows that God delivers. In fact, he is not just *a* deliverer, but *my* deliverer, says David. David had known very real fears: enemies without and anxieties within. The Lord had delivered him from them *all*. More fears would arise. He would doubtless be awake at night again with only his tears for comfort. But the Lord had delivered him in the past, and this gave David confidence for the future.

'Those who look to him are radiant.' This beautiful image speaks of the blessing of looking to the Lord: our eyes are brightened, our faces shine, our spirits are renewed. It's language that picks up on Moses' face when he'd met with the Lord on Mount Sinai. As Moses came down the mountain, his face was shining with the reflected glory of the Lord.

David was not on a mountaintop, but in a cave. Not a place of light and life, but of darkness and death. Yet even there, David could know that 'mountaintop' experience of joy and peace in the Lord – and this is true for all believers. Christians are like phosphorescent stones that glow beautifully and give light in the darkness, not because they have a source of light within them, but because they have drunk in the light of the sun.

—Selah—

Did you notice that David starts by recording his experience – he answered *me* – but then moves to address all the community: 'Those who look to him are radiant.' David expects his experience to be shared by all who look to the Lord. This is part of why he writes so many personal psalms. He expects his words to be ones that all the people can use, as they too look to the same God for refuge.

Don't we find that to be the case? Can we not say along with David, 'I sought the LORD, and he answered me'? If we are Christian believers today, it is because God heard and answered our prayer, he delivered us from our deepest need. This is our conversion story, but it's also our story every day – if we have eyes to see – as in a thousand ways God proves himself to be our provider and our deliverer, the one who makes our faces shine.

23

PSALM 34:6–7
He hears his people's cries

This poor man cried, and the Lord *heard him*
and saved him out of all his troubles.
The angel of the Lord *encamps*
round those who fear him, and delivers them.

The Lord hears his people's cries. Just pause for a moment to take in the wonder of this. This is one of the reasons David can praise God in all circumstances. God hears the prayers of his people; whether bold intercessions or lonely tears, the Lord hears them all.

'This poor man cried, and the Lord heard him.' The word 'poor' could also be translated 'lowly', 'needy' or even 'wretched'. This was a man at rock bottom. But the Lord heard David's cry. This is the same personal care that would be exemplified by Jesus Christ: the shepherd who would leave the ninety-nine to pursue the one lost sheep. This is a God who cares for little ones, for the weak, for the poor. Your prayers may not be loud or confident. Your voice may not be strong. But the Lord hears.

The words in these verses are personal, but as in verse five, David chooses language that links his experience with the narratives of the Exodus. When God's people were slaves in Egypt, needy and wretched, they cried out to God, and God heard their cries. He knew their sufferings and had compassion on them. And so he delivered them (Ex. 2:23–25; 3:7).

In his own experience, David sees the same strong hand and outstretched arm of the God of the Exodus. And also the same compassion. How his people are *matters* to God.

—Selah—

This is why in the next verse David again broadens out to include all the people. Again, he expects his own experience to be the people's experience. 'I was delivered,' says David. 'And you should expect to be too.'

'The angel of the Lord encamps round those who fear him, and delivers them.' Once God had rescued his people from Egypt, he led them through the desert of Sinai. This was a place where they were vulnerable, with the Egyptian army not far away, and no obvious places of shelter or security. Yet the Lord's angel encamped around them: a mighty barrier of protection that no-one could breach. The Lord's angel was with them on the journey, guarding and protecting them until they reached their journey's end: the promised land.

So too the angel of the Lord encamps around those who fear him today. We may feel like we're in a desert. We may feel vulnerable, without protection. We may be far from home and isolated. Earthly comforts may be very few indeed. But if we look with the eyes of faith, we'll see the flaming angcls on thc hilltops surrounding us, personally and purposefully guarding us. We'll see these 'ministering spirits sent to serve those who will inherit salvation' (Heb. 1:14, NIV). We'll see *the* angel of the Lord, Christ himself, who is ever with us and for us.

In times of trouble, look to God's actions in the past. Press these things down into your hearts and minds. Retell the story of the Exodus and expect God to act the same towards you today. The angel of the Lord encamps round you, right now, and every day until you enter the gates of glory.

24

PSALM 34:8 *Taste and see*

Oh, taste and see that the Lord is good!
Blessed is the man who takes refuge in him!

It's been said that the distance from the head to the heart is only 18 inches, yet it's also the longest journey we can take. Perhaps you've experienced that situation where you know certain truths about God, but you struggle to *delight* in those truths in your heart.

David has been piling up evidence from his own life of how God has been trustworthy. He has been showing that God is the God of the Exodus, the mighty, compassionate, promise-keeping God. But evidence can only get you so far. David now calls for those around him to 'taste and see that the Lord is good!' He wants them to know of the Lord's goodness, not just theoretically, but in their own experience.

I love the 'taste' metaphor here. It's so personal. I can read all about how a food tastes, but that will never be the same as actually trying it. And I cannot taste something from a safe distance. There is a commitment involved.

David is saying, 'You've heard all the evidence, you've seen a thousand times in Scripture that God is good and trustworthy. But now discover that experientially for yourselves. Come to him. Rely on him. Lean on him, and find that he is able to take your weight and hold you firm. Taste and see that he is good.'

—Selah—

In his first letter, the apostle Peter picks up this metaphor and describes Christian believers as those who have 'tasted that the Lord is good' (1 Pet. 2:3). Becoming a Christian was always about more than just getting our thinking straight about God. And the same is true for our growth in Christ. We need to keep tasting of the Lord's goodness.

Maybe that means surrendering some area of our life that we've been holding at arm's length from him. And as we do so, pray that we would taste and see that he is good.

Maybe it's turning to him in times of trial, not looking elsewhere for the refuge and comfort we need. And as we come to him and find him faithful, we maybe even taste his goodness in a unique way in this time of trial.

Maybe it's reading Scripture with this goal, praying each time we open the Bible, 'Lord please help me taste your goodness today.'

Maybe it's coming to him in prayer – for ourselves, but also for the needs of others – even if that's not our regular pattern. And as we do so, let that be an opportunity to taste and see the Lord's goodness.

David knows the Lord is good, not only from studying truths about God, but from his experience of God. 'Taste and see,' says David. Taste the Lord's goodness; experience his faithfulness, and know first-hand the great blessing of taking refuge in him.

25

PSALM 34:9–10
Lacking no good thing

Oh, fear the L*ORD, you his saints,*
for those who fear him have no lack!
The young lions suffer want and hunger;
but those who seek the L*ORD lack no good thing.*

'Those who seek the LORD lack no good thing.' These are wonderful words, and powerful truths. But some of us might take some persuading. We might think it's the sort of phrase that's easy to say when life is all going well, but is it really realistic in times when life has fallen apart?

But think of David's situation, and that of those around him. Everything in their circumstances pointed to the Lord *not* providing. The only reason they were there in the cave is because they were in debt or bitter in soul (1 Sam. 22:1–2). They were there because they lacked *so many* good things. Perhaps they lacked houses, they lacked employment, they lacked health, they lacked family to look after them. How can David say, 'those who seek the LORD lack no good thing' to *these* people? How can he say it to us?

Perhaps part of the answer is in how David describes believers. He describes them as those who 'seek the LORD' but also as those who '*fear* the LORD'. To fear the Lord is not to be in terror of him, but it is to have a big view of him; to see him as mighty and majestic, and submit ourselves to him.

If God were small, then perhaps our circumstances would prevail. A small god might make mistakes, might not know our needs, might not be able to provide. But we have no small god!

The God that David has come to know is one who is able to provide and deliver, even in the desert. The God that David serves is one whose plans are always good, even when David can't always see what God is doing. If God is bigger than my circumstances, then God is able to do me good, even in and through those circumstances. David fears God – which means he doesn't have to fear anything else.

—Selah—

Fear of the Lord puts everything else into perspective. The 'young lions' – David's way of referring to the powerful enemies he is fleeing from – look so sleek and mighty, yet they suffer want and hunger. Don't envy the rich, the powerful, the healthy, those with all the blessings that we might want. Without God they lack not just the greatest good – God himself – but also the ability to rightly enjoy all those other good things.

By contrast, God's people lack no good thing. We need to understand this rightly. Verse 19 of this psalm says, 'Many are the afflictions of the righteous.' So the verses today are not presenting God as a sort of genie, who grants our every wish (whether that would be good for us or not). But God is a Father who knows the needs of his children, and will not let them lack anything that will be for their good. Our God is the God of the Exodus. He wouldn't rescue us, only then to let us die in the wilderness. No, he lovingly sustains us, giving us our daily bread, every day of our journey. We lack *nothing* that is ultimately for our good.

Remember this, had any other condition been better for you than the one in which you are, divine love would have put you there.

(Charles Spurgeon)[5]

26

PSALM 34:11–14
Turn from evil and do good

Come, O children, listen to me;
I will teach you the fear of the Lord.
What man is there who desires life
and loves many days, that he may see good?
Keep your tongue from evil
and your lips from speaking deceit.
Turn away from evil and do good;
seek peace and pursue it.

In 2016, Forbes magazine polled over 700 people asking them to name in one word what they desire the most in life.[6] It will be no great surprise that 'happiness' topped the list, ahead even of money and freedom. We all want to be happy. And it was no different in David's day.

David says the route to happiness and the good life is to be found in godly living. David is following on from the previous verses where he spoke about 'fear of the Lord' – that is getting a right view of God. But as in the rest of the psalm, the route to growing in our relationship with God is not just about thinking right thoughts; it is also walking in God's ways.

David starts with the tongue, that most rebellious of our organs: 'Keep your tongue from evil.' This command is all the more important in our age of social media. From the safety of our computer keyboards we can so easily return evil for evil, say hurtful things about others, inflict deep wounds through unkind or thoughtless words. Not only is this wrong, it's not the route to happiness. As Spurgeon puts it, 'Men cannot spit forth poison without feeling some of the venom burning their own flesh.'[7]

The same is true of lying: 'Keep … your lips from speaking deceit.' Telling lies may temporarily make others think we are better than we are, or may increase our power or control. But, to borrow another image from Spurgeon, lying only stuffs our pillow with thorns, so we have no rest; we are constantly afraid of being found out.

True happiness is found in turning away from evil and doing good, seeking peace and pursuing it. Notice there is a turning away from evil – deliberately putting distance between us and temptation. But there is also a turning to good. Good deeds have a transformative power in helping us overcome temptation, as we 'taste and see' that God is good and that his ways are best.

—Selah—

'Do good,' says David, because that's the route to life and good days. But we'll only believe that and live that way if we realise that God is good, and that he can be trusted to provide; we do not need to resort to illicit means to try to secure our safety or satisfaction.

If we wonder if this talk of happiness coming through godly living is just 'Old Testament religion', we must remember that the apostle Peter quotes these very verses in his first letter, and applies them directly to Christian believers – and to us today (1 Pet. 3:10–12).

Walking God's way is the route to life and good days. Walking God's way is the route to knowing him better. That was David's experience. And, of course, that was Jesus' experience.

Jesus came that we might have life to the full. If we desire the life and good days that our saviour promises us, we must walk in the good paths our saviour lays before us.

27

PSALM 34:15
His ears towards their cry

The eyes of the Lord are towards the righteous
and his ears towards their cry.

I remember several years ago I was sitting in a café and at the table next to me was a young woman and her mother. The young woman was talking animatedly and pouring out her heart, but I could see that the mother was only pretending to listen, and was more interested in checking her phone. She was present *with* her daughter, but not really present *for* her daughter. It was heart-breaking.

Maybe we fear this is what God is like. Remote. Not interested. Even if he does hear our prayers, he doesn't really care. It would be really hard to delight in a god like that. It would be really hard to trust a god like that.

'The eyes of the Lord are towards the righteous.' God's face is turned towards his people, attentive to us. He knows all that we do, even before we tell him. None of our tears are hidden, none of our fears are concealed in the dark. God is never too caught up in his own business to care about our struggles.

God's eyes being towards us means more than just him knowing about us. Think of the priestly blessing in Numbers: the Lord's face is turned towards us to bless us, to keep us, to be gracious to us and to give us peace (Num. 6:24–26). His eyes are towards 'the righteous' – here just meaning 'his people' – to do us *good*.

'His ears towards their cry.' God hears our tidy prayers that begin 'O Lord' and end with a confident 'Amen'. But he also hears our jumbled mess and our wordless groans. His ears are turned towards us because he wants to hear it all.

—Selah—

David wants those around him to know the Lord's care of them and presence with them. This is how they'll be able to praise and trust God in all situations, even in times of trial like they are in. The same is true of us. But sometimes it's easier to believe these things in principle than really live as if they're true.

Previous generations of Christians spoke of living *Coram Deo* – a Latin phrase meaning 'before the face of God', or more simply 'in the presence of God'. Seek to remember the Lord's presence with us at all times. Try to be aware of him at each moment of the day.

We wake up. We do so in the presence of God, with his eyes upon us. Perhaps we have breakfast, with God's eyes towards us. We have our first conversations of the day and begin our work or activity. We do these with the eyes of the Lord towards us, and his ears turned to us. When we break for lunch or rest, God does not cease his loving attention to us. In our moments of doubt, or selfishness, or sin, his eyes are still upon us, he still longs for us to commune with him again. When we lay our head to rest and close our eyes in sleep, his eyes never close, but he keeps his watchful care over his children.

Oh, what griefs we'd spare ourselves, oh what rich draughts of comfort we'd drink, if we only meditated more on the eyes and the ears of the Lord, turned ever towards us in love.

28

PSALM 34:16
His face against evil

The face of the Lord *is against those who do evil,*
to cut off the memory of them from the earth.

I'll confess, I originally didn't have this as a separate devotion. It seemed too stark – and not the sort of thing to set us up for the day ahead. Perhaps that's your impression as you read it. But before moving to supposed greener pastures, let's try to hear these words in their original context, spoken to those with David in the cave.

David is surrounded by those who are in distress, in debt and bitter of soul. They are the marginalised, those mistreated by the powerful people at the centre who wanted rebellion: to overthrow Saul. But David encouraged them to keep trusting God; to turn from evil and do good; to seek peace and pursue it (vv. 13–14).

Then, as now, God's judgment on evil is a vital truth that enables suffering believers to keep going. All their circumstances suggested that God was not in control, that God didn't care about the way they were being mistreated. Many in our society today face similar circumstances, where evil seems to go unchecked. How tragic that during the 2020 lockdown in the UK, domestic violence increased, perhaps in part because there were no witnesses, no reckoning? It seems no-one sees and no-one cares.

But the face of the Lord 'is against those who do evil'. Just as the Lord is personally, purposefully present to bless his people (v. 15), so too he is personally, purposefully opposed to those who do evil. He will 'cut off the memory of them from the earth'.

What an encouragement for those who are persecuted. What comfort to those who suffer unjustly. God is not distant or uncaring. He is against all who do evil. It matters to God.

Those who perpetrate evil will not ultimately prosper. Those who seem to get away with it in this life *will* be brought to justice. Wickedness has no hope, no future. It will not endure.

—Selah—

This verse is a great encouragement for persecuted believers, but it warns us as well. God is God and is not to be trifled with. Evil is serious and is not to be dabbled in. We must not envy the wicked or think that we could safely turn from walking in God's paths to walking in wickedness.

God is resolutely opposed to all evil; he will cut off the memory of it from the earth. This verse corrects small views of God we may have, and it warns us against turning from him. This is not a God for whom sin and wickedness are trivial things. He is perfectly and wonderfully good, and *therefore* perfectly and wonderfully opposed to all evil.

Gloriously, there is full forgiveness for those who come to him; for those who trust in Jesus. Verse 15 celebrates the abundant comfort and security of those who trust in the Lord. But we need to see the other side. Verse 16 paints the abject hopelessness of trying to rebel against him.

Ponder both 'the kindness and the severity of God' (Rom. 11:22).

29

PSALM 34:17–18
Near to the broken-hearted

When the righteous cry for help, the LORD hears
and delivers them out of all their troubles.
The LORD is near to the broken-hearted
and saves the crushed in spirit.

As the psalm draws to its conclusion, David piles up the images of how God treats the righteous (highlighted by some contrasts with how he treats the wicked). David knows that for the suffering believers around him, they don't just need to know truths about God in general, but about how he is towards *them*. How does God treat his people?

It's no surprise that David returns to the theme of the Lord hearing his people's cries. Prayer is one of the chief blessings of the Christian life – not a duty to be performed, but a fellowship to be enjoyed and a privilege to delight in. Notice the unbroken chain here: the righteous pray, God hears, he delivers. As Spurgeon put it, 'Prayer moves the arm that moves the world.'[8]

David says that when the righteous pray, God 'delivers them out of all their troubles'. It is almost a word-for-word repeat of what David said of himself in verse 6. David expects his experience to be shared by all God's people.

David speaks of deliverance from *all* troubles. No pit is too deep, no enemy too strong, no night too dark, no grief too acute, no sin too shameful: the Lord delivers his people out of them all.

God's deliverance looks different in different situations. Sometimes that deliverance will look like Daniel's rescue from the lions. Sometimes it will look like Stephen's life, which was taken by cruel men with stones. But these men did not prevail; the worst they could do to Stephen only hastened him – face shining like an angel – into the blessed presence of his Lord.

—Selah—

Verse 18 develops this idea of deliverance, and how David can speak of deliverance from all troubles. Often in the psalms, the two parts of a verse are in parallel, saying very similar things. They build up a composite picture, like two subtly different camera angles on the same reality. Look at verse 18. The second half of the verse speaks of *salvation*, which is paralleled with the Lord being *near*.

What does it mean to be saved? It means to be near God! David is not just saying that God comes near so that he can save – though this is gloriously true. Salvation is never something God delegates from a distance. There is more: God coming near is what salvation itself consists in.

Salvation includes peace and security and protection. But none of these things are the heart of salvation. The heart and goal of salvation is closeness and intimacy with God himself.

This is what God has always been like for his people – a God who draws near. This is what led Christ to come into the world as Immanuel: God with us. This is what led the Father to pour out his Spirit into our hearts, so we would not be left as orphans.

Are you feeling broken-hearted? Is your spirit crushed? Know that God is near to you. Near, to hear your prayers. Near, to offer you comfort. Near, to protect from enemies. Near, to give you himself.

30

PSALM 34:19–20
Many afflictions

Many are the afflictions of the righteous,
but the LORD *delivers him out of them all.*
He keeps all his bones;
not one of them is broken.

'Many are the afflictions of the righteous.' How we need to hear these words. They correct two errors that are equally damaging as we seek to live our Christian lives. The first error is to think that becoming a Christian takes away all our afflictions *now*. Perhaps we've known people who've been damaged by false promises; when their life has become hard, they've believed that God has abandoned them.

The second, and related, error, is to think that if I am suffering, then I must have done something to deserve it. Maybe me finding life so hard is because I'm not trusting God enough, haven't surrendered fully enough to his will. Maybe my affliction is the sign of sin in my life.

But David says that even the righteous suffer affliction. The path of discipleship is a path of life, of joy, of radiant faces and of God's presence all the way. But it is also a hard path, one with enemies without and within.

Wasn't this how our saviour lived? *The* righteous one, who always fully obeyed. He always trusted his Father, always made the right decisions; he certainly couldn't be accused of lacking faith. Nor could we doubt the

Father's love for his son. Yet Jesus suffered afflictions. His was the way of the cross before resurrection. And all his people are to take up their cross and follow. The righteous will face afflictions, just as Christ the righteous one faced afflictions.

—Selah—

'But the LORD delivers him out of them all.' Afflictions never have the final word. God's people are secure. This is what the reference to no broken bones in verse 20 originally meant. Someone's 'bones' represented their inner being (cf. Ps. 6:2), so no bones being broken was a metaphor for security. Nothing can ultimately harm God's people. The worst Satan can do is inflict a flesh wound – a scratch. He can't cut us deep.

But, of course, these words found a very literal fulfilment as Jesus died on the cross, when none of his bones were broken. David's experience of innocent suffering in Psalm 34 points to the sufferings of Christ.

This is one of the reasons I love the psalms. David is both an example of what all believers will go through (which is how 1 Peter uses Psalm 34), but also a pattern of what Christ would go through (which is how John uses Psalm 34). In one psalm of David, we learn of the life of a believer, and we are pointed to our saviour.

Like Christ, we will face many afflictions as we seek to live for God in this world. But like Christ, we'll ultimately be delivered out of them all. Satan may wound us, but our bones will never be broken, our core identity will remain untouched.

When David wanted to reflect on the Lord's deliverance, he looked back to the empty Egyptian fields where the Israelites had been slaves. We look back to the empty tomb!

'Many are the afflictions of the righteous.' Take heart when things are hard. This is normal Christian living.

'But the LORD delivers him out of them all.' Could we expect anything less from a God who when he came into our world, took the name 'Jesus' – the Lord *saves*?

31

PSALM 34:21–22
No condemnation

Affliction will slay the wicked,
and those who hate the righteous will be condemned.
The LORD redeems the life of his servants;
none of those who take refuge in him will be condemned.

What do you need to know in order to live for God in this world – to praise God in all circumstances? That's really what all of Psalm 34 has been about. Part of the answer is to know where history is going. If we live as if this world and our current circumstances are all there are, we will be tempted to give up or turn away from trust in God. We need to see how the story ends.

'Affliction will slay the wicked.' For a little while now, living without God might seem like the path of blessing. But turning away from God is the most short-term of short-term strategies. It only leads to condemnation.

Notice the parallel in verse 21. The 'wicked' here are identified as those who 'hate the righteous'. But the word 'righteous' is a singular, meaning 'the righteous one'. Ultimately, whether you are counted among the righteous or the wicked depends on how you respond to Jesus, *the* righteous one.

It's possible to claim neutrality in many areas of life, but not in our response to Jesus. We are either for him, or against him. The wicked are those who reject Jesus. The righteous are not those who are morally perfect, but those who take refuge in him (cf. Ps. 2:12).

God has installed his king, Jesus, as ruler over all. We must not think we have any hope or any future if we oppose his rule. All evil will be done away with. Every last enemy will be brought under Jesus' feet.

—Selah—

By contrast, look how the Lord treats his servants. The psalm finishes with three powerful images to bind up the fainting hearts of believers.

He redeems them. Like the Exodus generation, God delivers his people out of cruel slavery. He pays the debt they owe. He carries them in his arms. He leads them to a land of rest. He brings them to himself.

He is their refuge. He is a place of safety, of shelter; a place where they can come to no harm. Whatever you face today, God is your refuge.

No condemnation. When history is rolled up and God comes to judge, we have nothing to fear. Nothing! We know this with even greater certainty than David did. The blood of Christ speaks 'a better word' (Heb. 12:24), a word of 'no condemnation' (Rom. 8:1), a word of sins fully paid, a word of life and peace and hope and a future.

Are you weighed down by sin?
There is no condemnation for those who are in Christ Jesus!
Do you find it hard to let go of the past?
There is no condemnation for those who are in Christ Jesus!
Do you hear Satan's accusations against you?
There is no condemnation for those who are in Christ Jesus!
Do you wonder whether God will accept you?
There is no condemnation for those who are in Christ Jesus!

We've read the last page of God's book. We know it ends well. And so we can keep going, keep praising.

32

PSALM 147:1 *It is good to praise*

Praise the L*ORD*!
For it is good to sing praises to our God;
for it is pleasant, and a song of praise is fitting.

Psalm 147 forms part of the 'great Hallelujah' at the end of the book of Psalms. Psalms 146–150 all begin and end with the command to 'Praise the LORD' – 'Hallelujah' in Hebrew.

Although it is a command, this call to praise is hardly a burdensome one. In calling us to praise, God is seeking what is best for us. It is good to sing praises. It is pleasant, it is fitting. It brings us joy! God is inviting us to know the good life.

Saying, 'Praise the LORD' is the biblical equivalent of saying, 'Open your eyes' to a child who has been sitting eyes closed while a birthday surprise is being prepared by her parents. When her parents say, 'Open your eyes!' we wouldn't see this as a duty or a burden. It is an invitation. So too the call to 'Praise the LORD' is an invitation to open our eyes to reality, to the joys that are right in front of us, if we could only see them.

This is why the rest of Psalm 147 catalogues reasons why God is to be praised. Though it might be called a 'praise' psalm, in fact the focus of the psalm is not on our praises, but on God himself. It would more properly be called a 'God is great' psalm!

Praise in and of itself is not the main thing. Rather, praise is good because of the *object* of our praise: God. In fact, the verse could be translated slightly differently, highlighting that it is God himself (not our praise) who is the focus:

'It is good to sing praises to our God, *for he is beautiful.*'

—Selah—

Maybe your heart feels cold. Some days you wake up and don't feel like praising. Perhaps very real cares and anxieties weigh down on you, and threaten to quench any small flame of love that flickers in your heart. Don't look within, don't try to tend to that flame; don't try to coax your heart into greater praise.

Look up! Gaze on the majesty of God, and let the light and heat of his goodness and beauty set your heart aflame once more. That's precisely what David will help us do through the rest of the psalm.

Did you also notice the reference to singing? Of course, praise and worship includes more than just singing, but the psalmist does assume that the call to praise and worship will always be a call to sing.

Singing gives opportunity to express how we feel about God – to pour out our adoration to him. But it does more than that. It also *shapes* us. It retunes our hearts. When we sing of the Lord's goodness and greatness, we present these truths again to our hearts and minds, and this is transformative. Our singing doesn't simply express our love for God; it is a means of kindling it into flame, and energising our whole lives of worship.

Praise the Lord! It is good and pleasant. It is *fitting* – it is the best way to live. Praise is a gift from God to us: a means by which we can have our eyes opened afresh to the wonders before us, and have our hearts lifted to the Lord's beauty.

33

PSALM 147:2–3
He gathers the outcasts

The Lord *builds up Jerusalem;*
he gathers the outcasts of Israel.
He heals the broken-hearted
and binds up their wounds.

Psalm 147 is a resounding call to 'Praise the Lord!' As we saw last time, such loud calls to praise are always accompanied by even louder celebrations of who God is and why he is worthy of praise. At the top of the list for the psalmist here is that God gathers those who are scattered, and brings home the lost. A God like that is worth praising!

Verse 2 has the return from exile in view. God's people had been in Babylon, cast out of the garden-land of Israel, cast far away from the presence of God in the temple. All this had happened because of their own sin. They seemed too far gone, too far lost. Yet the Lord – as he had always promised – gathered them back.

This is the glory of the God we worship. He is in the business of bringing people home. He is in the business of opening wide his arms so that even those who have wandered and strayed can find a welcome. Just as he built up the ancient ruins of Jerusalem, he builds up the ruins of our lives, bringing beauty where once there was only brokenness. No situation is too helpless for God.

You cannot have run too far. You cannot have strayed for too long. You cannot have sinned too deeply for *this* God to bring you home. He gathers the outcasts – even you and me.

—Selah—

What does he do when these outcasts arrive at home? Is he waiting with a stick to beat them? Is he there with a disapproving frown? Or is he simply distant – his love conditional on our performance, as has been the case with so many other people in our lives?

No, he 'heals the broken-hearted'. He 'binds up their wounds'. Perhaps these are the truths you most need to hear. Perhaps they are the truths you find hardest to believe.

Could there really be a God like that? Could there really be a God of such tender compassion? Could there really be a God who understands our trials and meets us in our need? Could God heal me after all I've done? After all that's been done to me?

When Christ stepped onto this earth, we saw most clearly what has *always* been true of our Lord God. He has always been a God of healing the broken-hearted and binding up wounds. It's what he *loves* to do.

In Christ, we saw this heart of God most perfectly and beautifully displayed. Jesus didn't just carry our sins on the cross, he bore our sorrows as well. He came to deal with the guilt that our sins deserve, but also the damage that sin brings in our lives. He came to restore and heal. He came to bring us home. Gently. Tenderly. By his wounds we are healed. By his broken-heartedness our hearts are made whole again.

34

PSALM 147:4–6
The number of the stars

He determines the number of the stars;
he gives to all of them their names.
Great is our Lord, and abundant in power;
his understanding is beyond measure.
The Lord lifts up the humble;
he casts the wicked to the ground.

In 2016, NASA announced that the universe contained 10 times more galaxies than had been previously thought.[9] New research suggested a total of 2 *trillion* galaxies. To put this into perspective, that's twenty galaxies for everyone who has ever lived – the overall number of stars being 1 septillion (1 with 24 zeroes).[10] If everyone who ever lived had spent their entire life naming stars at one per second, we'd still be less than 1% of the way towards naming all the stars. These numbers boggle our minds. Yet God determines the number of the stars. More than that, he *names* them. He knows them individually.

No wonder the psalmist continues, 'Great is our Lord, and abundant in power; his understanding is beyond measure.' The word 'measure' is the same as 'number' in verse 4. The number of stars is limited: it can be measured (by God at least). Whereas his understanding is beyond measure, it is limitless. Take the biggest thing we can conceive, and it is still far smaller, far less impressive than God himself.

This is a consistent theme in the psalms. The Lord is portrayed as so much bigger than we might think. Reading the psalms prevents us from having a small view of God, a view of God that is very tame and easy to understand. The psalms blow our minds with the utter transcendence of God. If our brains hurt when we try to think of numbers this big, or when we start to think more about the nature of our universe, how much more should we expect to be out of our depth when thinking about God the creator of all these things!

—Selah—

Did you notice the camera suddenly zoom in on verse 6? We've been considering the vast canopy of the heavens, and now we're focussed in very personal detail: 'The Lord lifts up the humble' (or afflicted).

The psalmist deliberately puts verses 5 and 6 together to show how staggering God's care for the afflicted is. The God with unlimited power uses it to oppose wickedness and care for the weak. The hands that fashioned the stars are the hands that washed the disciples' feet. The hands that stretched out the heavens are the hands that bind up the wounds of the broken – that bind up your wounds.

Great power is a terrifying thing in the wrong hands. We have seen that too well in world news in recent years. But look how the Lord uses his power: consistently to heal the broken-hearted and lift up the humble and afflicted.

If you are feeling fragile, if you fear that you might almost be at breaking point, the Lord will not break you. The one who knows all the movements of the stars also knows all the needs of his people. Fret not, little children, for you are worth more to him than many stars.

35

PSALM 147:7–9
God our provider

Sing to the Lord *with thanksgiving;*
make melody to our God on the lyre!
He covers the heavens with clouds;
he prepares rain for the earth;
he makes grass grow on the hills.
He gives to the beasts their food,
and to the young ravens that cry.

The next section of the psalm begins with the same pattern: a call to praise, and then reasons why God is to be praised. Here the reasons for praise are God's care for his creation. The dark clouds that mass in the west; the stillness and heaviness in the air, then the first drops of autumn rain that fall – these are all from the Lord. In the dry climate of Israel, without the Lord's provision in that way, there would be no harvest.

He makes the grass grow on the hills. These were the dry Judean hills with no natural sources of water. Barren and unpromising places. But even there, the Lord provides. No situation is too unpromising for the Lord to turn desert to pasture and barrenness to blessing.

God is a provider. He gives the beasts their food, whether cattle in the stalls or the young ravens in the field. I wonder if Jesus – who knew and loved the psalms – had this verse in view when he told his followers not to worry, and pointed them to God clothing the grass of the field and feeding the birds of the air.

The psalmist tells us to look at creation and learn of the Lord. His fingerprints are everywhere, his goodness is constantly on display. Scripture gives us the lenses to see this properly: when you see the clouds, when you see the rain, let that teach you that the Lord provides. Let that teach you the Lord cares. When you see an animal eating, when you see a bird pecking at its food, when the rain falls and the crops grow, say, 'The Lord is at work! The Lord is doing this!'

—Selah—

The psalmist sees God's care for creation as a reason to sing and make melody to God. And through the centuries many Christian hymns have done just that, picking up the sort of ideas expressed in these verses.

But I wonder if that trend is decreasing. I've noticed songs like 'How Great Thou Art' and 'Great is Thy Faithfulness' being sung omitting the verses that speak of God's care for creation. I understand the desire: to focus attention on redemption, and all Christ achieved for us on the cross. But Jesus' example is important for us: he told us to celebrate and learn from God's provision in the natural world.

There is no tension between creation and redemption. The one who is our redeemer is also the one through whom and for whom everything was made. The one who saved us also provides for us.

May we never lose sight of the salvation we have in Christ crucified. But may we never narrow down that salvation by separating it from God's ongoing provision for his people, and God's care for all of creation. What God has joined together, let us not separate. God cares for all of creation – and how much more does he care for us, his precious children. That's a reason for us to sing and make melody to him today.

36

PSALM 147:10–11
Not in the strength of the horse

His delight is not in the strength of the horse,
nor his pleasure in the legs of a man,
but the Lord *takes pleasure in those who fear him,*
in those who hope in his steadfast love.

If you walk into your local bookstore, you'll find shelves filled with books on productivity. A quick search on Amazon shows over 50,000 such titles, each one offering ways to maximise our effectiveness, our output and our success. We live in a society where our worth needs to be *earned*. Someone is valued to the extent that they are 'a productive member of society'. This may sound good to some of us. Until we find ourselves sick, or incapacitated in some way. Until we find ourselves unable to be 'productive' in ways that society values. What then of our value and worth?

And is it the same with God? Does he value us according to what we can contribute to his team? Do we have the talents or the wisdom to make a difference? Do we have the energy?

Our verses today flow naturally out of the vast doctrine of God that the psalm has been painting so far. And they show a God who operates radically differently to our society, and so radically differently to me.

So often our personal interactions are driven by our *needs*. I've seen the ugly spectre of this in my own life. If I'm feeling a bit bored, I look for a good conversationalist. If I'm needing comfort, I look for someone with a listening ear. If I'm trying to progress in my business, I keep my eye out for people who may have contacts that help me along.

But how different God is. God has no needs. He is the star-namer and life-giver. He does not need you or me.

He doesn't need to look to 'the strength of the horse' – here most likely the war horse – to win his battles. He doesn't look to 'the legs of a man' – that is to human strength. He doesn't need any of those things. He is utterly sufficient in himself. No person, no church, no institution is indispensable in God's kingdom.

—Selah—

So what *does* God want from us? He wants us to fear him – that is to see him as great and glorious, and to hope in his steadfast love. He wants us to remember that he's the God who names the stars in a trillion galaxies, and then start living out the implications of this. He's not wowed by our gifts (and who gave us them anyway?). He's not more pleased with those who have high energy and high capacity. He doesn't value the 'healthy' more than those with severe disabilities or mental illnesses. In fact, when he stepped onto this earth, God came not to the healthy, the wealthy and the strong, but to the weak. He doesn't need us, and that is utterly liberating.

In the words of Francis Schaeffer, to God there are 'no little people'.[11] The Lord doesn't delight in our strength. The Lord doesn't delight in the effectiveness of our church's evangelistic publicity. His pleasure is not in the influence we have, the eloquence with which we speak. He doesn't delight in the qualifications we hold, the followers we have or our strategic importance for the kingdom of God. Rather, he 'takes pleasure in those who fear him', 'who hope in his steadfast love'.

If you're a Christian believer, he takes pleasure in you. Not because he wants something from you – your time, your energy, your gifts or your talents. But because he wants to give something to you: his steadfast love.

37

PSALM 147:12–14 *He satisfies us*

Praise the Lord, O Jerusalem!
Praise your God, O Zion!
For he strengthens the bars of your gates;
he blesses your children within you.
He makes peace in your borders;
he fills you with the finest of the wheat.

These verses give a picture of what it was like to live within the city of God. Gates strengthened: that is enemies kept away. Your children blessed within you: that is security and longevity, hope for the future. Peace in your borders: you are satisfied, you have every good thing. For a time in Jerusalem, it was like that. Under the reign of Solomon, there was a brief golden age of peace and prosperity. For centuries afterwards, the people would look back to those days with longing – those days when everyone sat under their own fig tree or vine and they ate and drank and were happy.

The psalmist is evoking those glory days of Jerusalem and saying they are a picture of life in the kingdom of God. It is a picture of where history is going: the glorious future city we await, the *new* Jerusalem, coming down out of heaven, where we will know peace, security and blessing for evermore. We look forward to a city that will make Solomon's Jerusalem look pale and dim, to peace and prosperity that will make even the best of this life look dull by comparison.

Though we are pilgrims here on earth, this psalm lifts us to heaven to view our glorious inheritance. Stay a while and view the landscape. Strain your ears to hear the angel songs. Fill your heart with blessed thoughts of the journey's end.

—Selah—

The ultimate fulfilment of these words is in the new creation, but as God's people we begin to experience these realities *now*. What made Jerusalem special was God's presence within her, and that's what we know as God's people today by his Spirit.

He strengthens the bars of your gates. We know the security of the loving arms of protection of God himself, keeping us safe. We have our saviour's words: 'no one will snatch them out of my hand' (John 10:28).

He blesses your children within you. Can there be any greater blessing for our children than being brought up in a home with Jesus at the centre? But our family is no longer now just physical. Whether we are married or not, whether we have children or not, we are all part of a spiritual family. In the church, we are all blessed with mothers and brothers and children. In the church, none should be left without 'children' to care for them in their old age.

He makes peace in your borders. Though imperfect, the church is a place where barriers are broken down, where people who are very different can be united and form one family. We also have an inner peace: no longer restlessly striving, but content in the Lord. Most importantly, we have peace with God.

He fills you with the finest of the wheat. Coming to God is never second best. I love it that when Jesus fed the 5000 in Matthew 14, everyone ate and they were *satisfied*. When we come to Jesus, we never go away disappointed. We never find Jesus to be lacking. He satisfies us with the finest of wheat – and so many other blessings besides – but the greatest gift he gives us is himself. We are satisfied in him.

38

PSALM 147:15–18
He sends the snow

He sends out his command to the earth;
his word runs swiftly.
He gives snow like wool;
he scatters hoarfrost like ashes.
He hurls down his crystals of ice like crumbs;
who can stand before his cold?
He sends out his word, and melts them;
he makes his wind blow and the waters flow.

My daughter is currently learning French, and I've been reminded of the different conventions for how we speak of the weather. Maybe you remember these if you ever studied French. In English, we say, 'It *is* cold.' In French, you don't use the word for 'is'; you use the word for 'do': 'Il *fait* froid.' So I remind my daughter to use the word 'do' not 'is' when speaking of the weather.

The psalmist also wants us to think differently when we talk about the weather: *God sends* the cold. The weather, indeed all of creation, is directed by God's word. God sends his command to the earth and these things happen. Look out of the window and what do you see? God sending clouds, or rain, or sun.

I love the poetry and beauty of this part of the psalm. The psalmist celebrates everything that happens as part of the wonderful (and at times mysterious) activity of God in the world.

We so often struggle with the fact that we can't see God, so we think of him as distant and remote. How that would change if even in this simple aspect of the weather we spoke differently. We check the weather forecast at the breakfast table: 'God is sending rain later.' We look out of the window: 'God's given us sun again today!'

Imagine how we'd be shaped if every day we spoke of the weather as the psalmist does here, and celebrated the active work of God in the world by his word.

—Selah—

As well as celebrating God's hand in giving weather, there is a metaphorical sense to these words too. The cold and frost and ice are symbols of some of the harder times in life. The times when we don't see the sun, when things are darker.

Perhaps some of us are facing such things right now, or have loved ones that are. Times of cold. Times of snow hiding and burying, like a blanket, so much of what normally makes life appealing.

The strange message of this psalm is that the Lord sends these things. He gives the snow. He sends the ice. Nothing takes place outside of his control.

This may be a hard truth to understand. But it is so much more comforting than the alternative, which is a God who is not in control of these things. We only have to read on into verse 18 to see that the God who sent the snows can also melt them. No season of life is outside of God's control. No winter is too deep, no night too dark, for God to be able to bring life again.

God is active in every aspect of this world – even when at times that seems perplexing. God sent the winter, and that means he is also able to bring the spring.

39

PSALM 147:19–20
He declared his word

He declares his word to Jacob,
his statutes and rules to Israel.
He has not dealt thus with any other nation;
they do not know his rules.
Praise the LORD!

The psalmist has been piling up reasons to praise the Lord. He is the God who names the stars. He is near to the broken-hearted. He provides for all things, and gives everything life and breath. He strengthens and blesses his people. Every aspect of creation, even the weather each day, is under his personal care.

But for the psalmist, the *climax* of all this is that God has declared his word to Jacob, and his statues to Israel. The high point of the psalmist's praise is reserved for the fact that God has spoken to his people. The reason for this is because of who God is.

If he is the God of such majesty and might, yet is so tender and compassionate towards his people, isn't he someone you want to listen to? If he is the one who names the stars and whose understanding is beyond measure, don't you think he is someone who can help us navigate this world we live in? If he is the one who provides for all the animals and beasts, and satisfies his people with the richest of food, don't you want to feed on the most satisfying food of his word to you? The word by which you are nourished to grow in the Christian life.

—Selah—

More than that, look at what happens when God speaks: God is *acting*. God 'sends out his command to the earth', and things happen (v. 15). 'God sends out his word', and the ice and frost melt (v. 18). God's word is the 'sceptre' of his kingdom, the instrument of his rule. Just as God created all things (those countless galaxies) by his word, so he directs and governs all things by his word.

But perhaps most significant of all, God speaks to his people because he wants *relationship* with them. The words 'statutes' and 'rules' may make us think just of commands, but these are *covenant* words that remind us of God's relationship with his people. As J.I. Packer famously put it, when God speaks, he is 'making friends' with us.[12] The Scriptures all point us to Christ, and lead us to life and joy in him.

The psalmist wants to lift our eyes to the extraordinary privilege of having God's word – of having a God who speaks because he wants *relationship* with us. In an age when we may have multiple Bibles round the house and even on our phones, we need to remember what a treasure we hold in our hands.

When you open your Bible, remember what happens when God speaks. Stars are born. Worlds are made. God's power is at work. And now he's about to speak to you, with no less power and no less purpose.

When you open your Bible, remember that God is speaking to *you*, because he wants relationship. He wants to build up Jerusalem, to gather outcasts, to heal the broken-hearted, to satisfy his people. These are the words that lift you to heaven. Treasure the Scriptures, because in them the Lord gives you himself.

40

PSALM 147:20b *Praise the Lord!*

Praise the L*ORD!*

Psalm 147 ends as it began: 'Praise the LORD!' We have seen that this call to praise is not a burdensome one, but an invitation to lift our eyes, lift our hearts and lift our voices to magnify the Lord's beauty. Praise and worship is what we were made for – it is what it is to be human. To praise the Lord is to live the right way up. To live with our eyes open. To see things as they are. Praising God is our duty, but also our delight!

In previous centuries, sailors could navigate the dark and stormy waters of the Atlantic Ocean by keeping their eyes on the North Star. Everything else around them moved, including the other stars, but the North Star was unchanging; if they fixed their view on that, everything else found its place. So too Christians can navigate all the uncertainties of this world by having our North Star in place: God first in our affections, and the object of our praise and worship. Only then will everything else make sense.

—Selah—

Praise is not simply what we were made for in the beginning. It is also where all history ends: in ceaseless praise to our saviour.

Revelation pictures the glorious future we await as one where Christ is praised amid his people. Everything is moving towards this destination, and this journey is prefigured in the psalms. Though they have had many dark valleys along the way, they end with a series of Hallelujah psalms, of which Psalm 147 is one. As this particular psalm concludes, and as the book of Psalms concludes, the volume has been turned up, and God is praised with full voice and glad hearts.

The reasons for praise will be all that this and other psalms have celebrated: the character of God, in particular his saving care for his people:

Praise the Lord, for he is star-namer; joy-maker; mountain-raiser;
He is lamb-gatherer; foot-washer; tear-bottler;
prayer-answerer; joy-bringer; comfort-speaker;
outcast-gatherer; heart-healer; wound-binder.

Praise the Lord because he is our light and our life,
our portion and our cup
our salvation and stronghold,
our greatest and highest joy.

Praise the Lord because he is ours and we are his for ever!

What have you seen in these four psalms that are reasons to praise the Lord? What images are most precious to you?

Why not read through these four psalms again, looking for descriptions of God that call forth our praise, and turning each of these to prayer.

ACKNOWLEDGMENTS

I am indebted to many people for helping shape the thoughts on these psalms, but in particular to C.J. Mahaney and Jeff Purswell. I heard C.J. Mahaney speak on Psalm 27 in January 2017, and was profoundly affected by those two sermons, which I've listened to again on recordings. The devotions on Psalms 27:4, 27:13 and 27:13 all owe a particular debt to these sermons, both in overall tone but also in some of the phrases used. I'm also grateful to Jeff Purswell for insights into Psalm 16 from a sermon of his that I listened to.

I greatly enjoyed too listening to Mike Cain's video devotions on the psalms during the 2020 lockdown, and my teaching of the psalms has benefitted hugely from his insights and approach.

- https://www.sgclouisville.org/sovereign-grace-church-louisville-sermons/sermon/2017-01-01/a-new-years-resolution-c-j-mahaney-psalm-27
- https://www.sgclouisville.org/sovereign-grace-church-louisville-sermons/sermon/2017-01-08/a-new-years-expectation-c-j-mahaney-psalm-27:7-14
- https://www.sgclouisville.org/sovereign-grace-church-louisville-sermons/sermon/2016-01-24/unshakable-and-everlasting-jeff-purswell-psalm-16
- https://www.youtube.com/watch?v=bbSOfeu83NM&list=PL-wNzc7pEYp8X6OQbZPaW6MZeekkBLx8D

ENDNOTES

1 Thomas Brooks, *Precious Remedies Against Satan's Devices* (first published 1652).

2 Anne Ross Cousin, 'The Sands of Time are Sinking' (1857).

3 J.I. Packer, *Knowing God* (London: Hodder & Stoughton, 1973), pp. 187, 184.

4 Derek Kidner, *Psalms 1–72* in the Tyndale Old Testament Commentaries series (Leicester: IVP, 1973), p. 122.

5 Charles H. Spurgeon, *Morning and Evening* (first published 1866), taken from the evening devotion for 11 November.

6 https://www.forbes.com/sites/kathycaprino/2016/05/24/the-top-8-things-people-desperately-desire-but-cant-seem-to-attain – accessed 30 March 2020.

7 Charles H. Spurgeon, *The Treasury of David, Volume 1* (Peabody, Mass: Henrickson, 2011), p. 125.

8 Taken by Charles H. Spurgeon's collection of sermons in the Metropolitan Tabernacle Pulpit (MTP 41:524).

9 https://www.nasa.gov/feature/goddard/2016/hubble-reveals-observable-universe-contains-10-times-more-galaxies-than-previously-thought – accessed 30 March 2020.

10 https://www.esa.int/Science_Exploration/Space_Science/Herschel/How_many_stars_are_there_in_the_Universe – accessed 30 March 2020.

11 Francis A. Schaeffer, *No Little People* (Wheaton, Illinois: Crossway, 1974).

12 J.I. Packer, *Knowing God* (London: Hodder & Stoughton, 1973), p. 39.